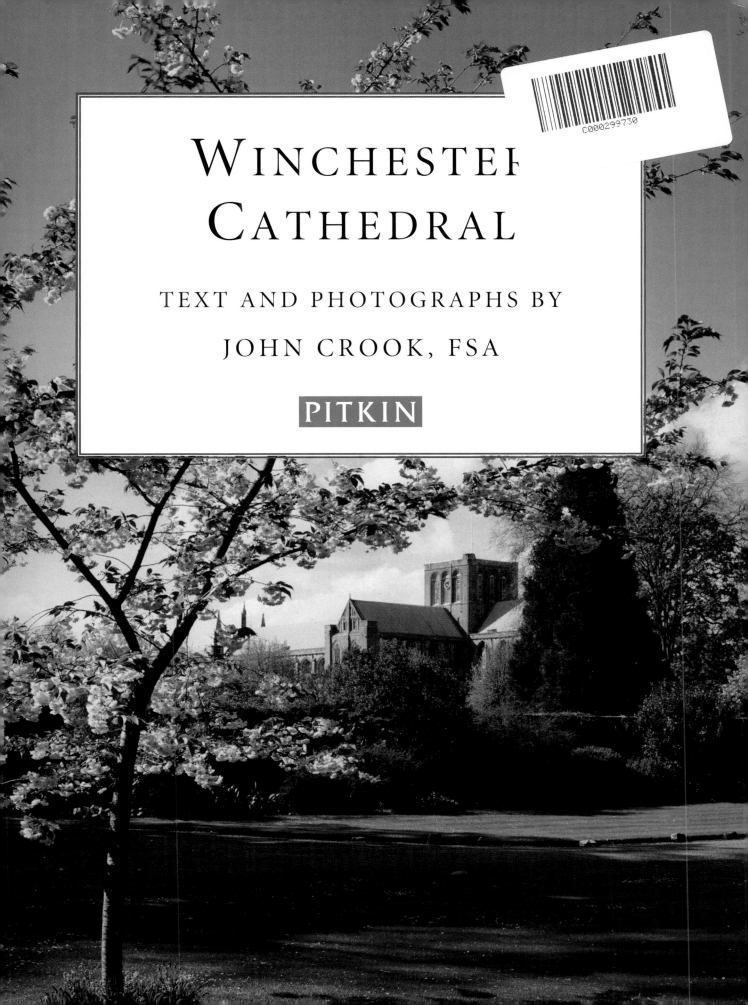

WINCHESTER CATHEDRAL

TEXT AND PHOTOGRAPHS BY

JOHN CROOK, FSA

PITKIN

Text written by John Crook. The author has asserted his moral rights.
Designed by Simon Borrough.
Plan created by Angela Lumley.
Plan inset based on an original drawing by John Crook.

All photographs © John Crook, except p.78 (Chapter of Winchester/John Crook).

Publication in this form © Pitkin Publishing 2016.

ISBN 978-1-84165-063-3   2/16

Pitkin Publishing, The History Press, The Mill, Brimscombe Port, Stroud, Gloucestershire, GL5 2QG.

Enquiries and sales: 01453 883300
Email: sales@thehistorypress.co.uk
www.thehistorypress.co.uk
Printed in India

FOREWORD

Like the porter in the monastery which once was here, this foreword is to welcome you into the discovery of this cathedral and its long and living story.

It is an axiom of our lives that visitors are to be welcomed as 'God's guests': that says it all.

It is as such that I welcome you at the outset of your exploration of Winchester Cathedral through these pages.

Michael Till

Michael Till
Dean of Winchester

CONTENTS

THE SAXON AND
ROMANESQUE CATHEDRALS

Nine hundred years is an impressive period for any building to remain in continuous use for its original purpose, but Winchester Cathedral goes back in time by half as much again. The present cathedral is the direct descendant of a small Anglo-Saxon church, later called Old Minster, which was built *c.*648, some 14 years after the arrival of St Birinus, apostle to the West Saxons. By 676, perhaps earlier, it was a cathedral, housing the throne (*cathedra*) of the bishop of the West Saxon diocese; three centuries later it was enlarged by Bishop Æthelwold (963–84) to accommodate a community of Benedictine monks imported from Abingdon, where he had previously been abbot, and ultimately from the monastery of Fleury on the Loire, one of the centres of the 10th-century monastic reform movement. Thus by the year 1000 Old Minster was a multi-purpose building. It was both a cathedral and a priory church; it was also a place of pilgrimage to the relics of St Swithun, a hitherto obscure 9th-century bishop of Winchester whose cult dated from 971, when Æthelwold elevated his remains into an opulent reliquary given by King Edgar. Finally, it had long been the last resting place of many West Saxon kings – though not King Alfred and his family, who were buried in neighbouring New Minster. In the early 11th century Cnut and his dynasty appear to have appropriated the east end of Old Minster as a royal mausoleum.

◀ OLD MINSTER, THE ANGLO-SAXON PREDECESSOR OF THE PRESENT CATHEDRAL, WAS EXCAVATED IN THE 1960S, AND ITS PLAN IS MARKED OUT IN THE CHURCHYARD NORTH OF THE NAVE. THE ORIGINAL CRUCIFORM CHURCH OF C.648 IS INDICATED IN RED BRICK.

▲ THE BONES OF PRE-CONQUEST MONARCHS AND BISHOPS, ONCE BURIED IN OLD MINSTER, LIE IN RENAISSANCE-STYLE MORTUARY CHESTS ON THE SCREENS EITHER SIDE OF THE HIGH ALTAR AREA. THE FOUR ORIGINAL CHESTS DATE FROM C.1525.

ALTHOUGH WINCHESTER LIES IN A RIVER VALLEY AND HAS GREATLY
EXPANDED SINCE THE MIDDLE AGES, THE CATHEDRAL REMAINS A PROMINENT
FEATURE OF THE VIEW OF THE CITY FROM ST CATHERINE'S HILL.

▼ A MODERN ICON OF ST SWITHUN, ONE OF THE CATHEDRAL'S PATRON SAINTS, BY SERGEI FYODOROV. AT THE TIME OF ÆTHELWOLD'S MONASTIC REFORMS A 9TH-CENTURY BISHOP, SWITHUN, WAS RECOGNIZED AS A SAINT, AND THE MONASTERY LATER BECAME KNOWN AS ST SWITHUN'S PRIORY.

▶ A STATUE OF BISHOP ÆTHELWOLD FROM THE GREAT SCREEN. ST ÆTHELWOLD WAS RESPONSIBLE FOR INTRODUCING A COMMUNITY OF BENEDICTINE MONKS INTO OLD MINSTER IN AROUND 964. ST SWITHUN'S PRIORY, AS IT WAS LATER CALLED, REMAINED A BENEDICTINE MONASTERY UNTIL 1539.

After the Battle of Hastings William the Conqueror's first concern was to be anointed king at Westminster, where Edward the Confessor's new abbey church symbolized the royal authority claimed by William. But Winchester remained the chief town of the realm: William constructed the castle and extended the royal palace over land confiscated from New Minster, whose monks had allegedly fought for Harold at Hastings. Meanwhile Winchester's last Saxon bishop, the pluralist Archbishop Stigand, was deposed in 1070. In his place William nominated his own royal chaplain, Walkelin, a secular canon from Rouen Cathedral and an able administrator: a political figure as much as a churchman, reflecting the role of the church as a central force in the new Anglo-Norman kingdom, as it already was in ducal Normandy.

For a time it looked as though the St Swithun's monks might be replaced by a college of canons, the set-up with which Walkelin was familiar. He even appointed 40 seculars as the new cathedral body. But Archbishop Lanfranc had by now been won over to English ways; thanks to his intervention the cathedral priory was spared. Walkelin's brother, Simeon, was appointed prior. Plans were drawn up to replace the Anglo-Saxon cathedral by an even larger church in the Norman Romanesque style which Edward the Confessor had pioneered at Westminster Abbey.

By the time work began on the new cathedral in 1079 sources of building materials had been organized. Old Minster had been built of oolitic limestone from the West Country, but an excellent stone was available locally. Quarr stone occurs near the north-east shore of the Isle of Wight, whence it could easily be shipped to the head of Southampton Water then overland to Winchester. Timber came from Hampshire's extensive oak-woods, and its supply is recalled in the story of the king's grant of as many trees as could be felled in three days and nights in nearby Hempage Wood. Walkelin allegedly assembled an army of 'carpenters', who stripped the wood bare. 'Have I gone mad?' asked the king, surveying the devastation. 'Surely I had a most delightful wood near Winchester?' The bishop was quickly pardoned. A later legend claimed that one token tree was left, the so-called 'Gospel Oak'.

▲ THE CRYPT, WITH ITS GROIN VAULTING SUPPORTED BY MASSIVE ROMANESQUE PILLARS, IS
THE LEAST ALTERED PART OF THE NORMAN CATHEDRAL OF BISHOP WALKELIN (1070 – 98).
THE WINTER FLOODING WAS PROBABLY NOT ORIGINALLY ANTICIPATED.

The foundations of the new church were laid out immediately south of Old Minster, which remained standing until the essential parts of its successor were ready. Intended as a symbol of Norman domination, Walkelin's cathedral was for a few years the longest church north of the Alps: 164m (534ft) overall. Its plan resembles that of contemporary churches in Normandy – scarcely surprising, as Walkelin was a canon of Rouen while that cathedral was under construction. So an 'apse-and-ambulatory' design was chosen (still apparent in the crypt), with a curved processional path around the head of the choir. At the west end of the nave, probably not completed until *c.*1120, twin towers flanked a tribune gallery overlooking the nave. This gallery, similar to those surviving at the ends of the transepts, may have been intended for the king to preside in state over his people during his Winchester visits, just as he had done in Old Minster, where William I 'wore his crown' at Easter whenever he was in England.

First to be built was the crypt, which is still one of the most evocative parts of the great church. It now floods almost every winter, but the floor level must have been determined during a dry spell: the seasonal flooding, which prevented liturgical use, cannot have been envisaged. Walkelin's crypt is similar to the 11th-century crypt of Rouen Cathedral, and both had a well: Winchester's was located directly beneath the high altar, symbolizing the living water of the Christian faith.

▶ THE MULTI-PHASE NATURE OF
THE CATHEDRAL IS EVIDENT FROM
THE NORTH-EAST: THE NORTH
TRANSEPT OF 1079 – 93 WITH
AISLE WINDOWS REMODELLED
IN THE 14TH CENTURY, THE
REBUILT TOWER OF C.1110, THE
RETROCHOIR (EARLY 13TH-
CENTURY), THE PRESBYTERY (14TH-
CENTURY), AND THE PRESBYTERY
AISLES (EARLY 16TH-CENTURY).

The transepts give the best idea of the internal appearance of Walkelin's cathedral, for all other parts have been rebuilt or remodelled above pavement level. The nave elevations originally resembled those still seen in the transepts, with three equal storeys: main arcade, gallery, and clerestory. Probably open to the rafters, or with a flat wooden ceiling, the nave would have seemed loftier than it does now. To enter the immense Winchester nave, with its rugged, cliff-like elevations, before they were tamed by William of Wykeham's Gothic remodelling, must have been a powerful experience for medieval pilgrims. By April 1093 the monks'

choir, the central tower, and a few bays of the nave were sufficiently complete for the brethren to make their ritual entrance, a ceremony attended by 'almost all the bishops and abbots in the land'. A first dedication presumably occurred, but there is no record that William Rufus was present. Then, on St Swithun's Day (15 July) the community processed back to Old Minster to collect that saint's reliquary, and the very next day Walkelin ordered the destruction of the old church, which occupied the site of the west end of the nave. Recycled stone from Old Minster supplemented Quarr limestone as the Norman cathedral was completed.

▲ THE TRANSEPTS GIVE THE BEST IMPRESSION OF BISHOP WALKELIN'S LATE
11TH-CENTURY CATHEDRAL. BEFORE IT WAS REMODELLED IN THE LATE 14TH CENTURY
THE NAVE WOULD HAVE LOOKED VERY SIMILAR, WITH A THREE-STOREY ELEVATION
CONSISTING OF MAIN ARCADE, GALLERY, AND CLERESTORY.

◀ THE ALARMING SOUTHWARD
LEAN OF THE SOUTH TRANSEPT
GABLE WALL IS A CONSEQUENCE OF
THE DIFFICULTY OF ESTABLISHING
SECURE FOUNDATIONS IN THIS
PART OF WINCHESTER. THE TOWER
COLLAPSED IN 1107 AND WAS
REBUILT SHORTLY AFTERWARDS.

▲ THE PURBECK MARBLE TOMB
NOW BENEATH THE TOWER WAS
WRONGLY THOUGHT TO BE THAT OF
WILLIAM RUFUS AND ORIGINALLY
STOOD IN FRONT OF THE HIGH
ALTAR. IT IS IN FACT THAT OF
BISHOP HENRY OF BLOIS, RUFUS'S
NEPHEW, AND WAS MOVED TO ITS
PRESENT POSITION IN 1886.

The abandoning of Old Minster meant that most of its prestigious burials had to be transferred to Walkelin's cathedral, though a few remained in place in a new 'memorial court' around Swithun's empty grave. It is thought that the stone sarcophagi containing more recent royal burials from Old Minster, notably Cnut and his family – together with two Normans, Duke Richard of Normandy (a son of William I, killed in the New Forest) and Earl Bjorn, William's kinsman – were placed on the low wall supporting the choir arcade piers. The tomb of Harthacnut and the double burial of Duke Richard and Earl Bjorn still occupy roughly the same position, having been moved only slightly in the 14th century. The bones of earlier monarchs and bishops may have been placed in the crypt; in the mid-12th century they would receive more fitting treatment.

The only king to be buried from the outset in Winchester Cathedral was William Rufus, who like his elder brother Richard also perished while hunting in the New Forest. Rufus was interred, apparently with little ceremony, beneath the tower. No bishop was present, Walkelin having recently died, and the funeral was conducted by Prior Godfrey. The monument known since the late 16th century as the 'Rufus Tomb' is now thought to be that of Bishop Henry of Blois, and was placed beneath the tower only in 1886.

Construction of the new cathedral did not run smoothly. There were subsidence problems in the transepts, and a modification to the original design, the addition of corner towers, was soon abandoned: the foundations would not bear the weight. Then in 1107 the central tower collapsed. This was quickly blamed on the Red King's grave beneath it, though the contemporary historian William of Malmesbury, despite his obvious distaste for Rufus, suspected poor workmanship. The new tower piers were thickened up, and the early 12th-century work is more accomplished than that of 20 to 30 years earlier: the stones are better cut and more finely jointed, and elegant 12th-century chevron decoration is visible in the tower. Originally this was a lantern tower open to the roof and all this decorative work could have been seen from the choir below. The down-draught must have been considerable, and in 1243 the monks obtained papal permission to wear caps in choir during cold weather.

By now William Giffard was bishop. He had previously been William Rufus's chancellor, and though Henry I nominated him to the see in 1100 he was not consecrated for seven years, holding out against Henry over the king's claim to invest bishops with their staff and ring. The Winchester monks were also in dispute with Giffard over land ownership. They accused the bishop of appropriating their rightful revenues and allegedly held a protest march, processing anti-clockwise around the cathedral, their crosses held upside down. Only *c.*1125 were relations healed: Giffard did penance in the Chapter House and placed a deed of restitution on the high altar. The chronicler assures us that he ended his days as an exemplary head of the monastery, taking his midday rest in the monks' dormitory, eating at the lowest table in the refectory, and dying in the infirmary. This enthusiasm for the monastic life also found expression in his founding of England's first Cistercian abbey, at Waverley, Surrey.

▲ THE 12TH-CENTURY TOWER WAS ORIGINALLY AN OPEN LANTERN TOWER, AND THE FINE INTERIOR DETAILING, INCLUDING CHEVRON MOULDING TYPICAL OF THE PERIOD, WOULD ORIGINALLY HAVE BEEN VISIBLE FROM THE CHOIR BELOW.

▶ THE GATES AT THE TOP OF THE STEPS FROM THE SOUTH TRANSEPT TO THE PRESBYTERY AISLE WERE ADAPTED FROM MEDIEVAL SCREENS. THIS SURVIVAL IS ONE OF THE EARLIEST EXAMPLES OF DECORATIVE IRONWORK IN ENGLAND, AND DATES FROM THE 12TH CENTURY.

▶ THE GATES AT THE TOP OF THE STEPS FROM THE SOUTH TRANSEPT TO THE PRESBYTERY AISLE WERE ADAPTED FROM MEDIEVAL SCREENS. THIS SURVIVAL IS ONE OF THE EARLIEST EXAMPLES OF DECORATIVE IRONWORK IN ENGLAND, AND DATES FROM THE 12TH CENTURY.

▲ A SUPERB MID-12TH-CENTURY CAEN STONE CAPITAL NOW DISPLAYED IN THE TRIFORIUM GALLERY SHOWS A BATTLE BETWEEN MYTHICAL BEASTS: CENTAURS, A GRIFFIN, AND A BASILISK. IT PROBABLY CAME FROM ONE OF THE DEMOLISHED PRIORY BUILDINGS, POSSIBLY THE INFIRMARY CLOISTER. THIS HIGH-QUALITY WORK DATES FROM THE TIME OF BISHOP HENRY OF BLOIS (1129–71).

It was during the final years of Giffard's episcopate that a Winchester monk, Reginald, crossed the North Sea bearing an arm-bone of St Swithun; with this relic he consecrated the future cathedral of Stavanger. Links with Stavanger were revived in 1962, the 1100th anniversary of Swithun's death, when his empty grave at Winchester was marked by a slab of Norwegian limestone.

An even greater man than Giffard was to become bishop. In 1129 Henry of Blois, aged about 30, was nominated. Three years previously his uncle Henry I had summoned him from the influential abbey of Cluny to be Abbot of Glastonbury. Bishop Henry had trained as a monk at Cluny, gaining a reputation as an able administrator. He was the son of Stephen, Count of Blois, and Adela, the Conqueror's daughter; his elder brother was King Stephen (1135–54). Bishop Henry played an important part in the civil wars of Stephen's troubled reign, supporting first his brother then, after Stephen's capture at Lincoln, his cousin Matilda.

Henry of Blois is remembered for his artistic patronage. His interest in the arts is shown in the story of how he bought antique statues during one of his visits to Rome. The bishop accumulated a wealth of art treasures during his travels, donating them to his cathedral, where two bays of the south transept aisle were walled off *c.*1160 to form a treasury. Most of Bishop Henry's Winchester projects date from after his return in 1158 from four years' voluntary exile at Cluny. In that year he is said to have raised the bodies of kings and bishops around the high altar: the apse was remodelled and a 'feretory platform' was created, upon which the reliquary of St Swithun could be more prominently displayed. Beneath the platform a short tunnel, the 'Holy Hole', led westwards from the ambulatory, allowing pilgrims closer access to the relics. As for the royal and episcopal bodies, Bishop Henry's concern seems to have been to place them under the close protection of the saint's remains. Two groups of bodies were involved. The first comprised early kings and bishops of Wessex, whose bodies may have mouldered in the crypt in unmarked sarcophagi since Old Minster was demolished; these bones were placed all together, 'kings with bishops, and bishops with kings', in lead caskets around the Holy Hole. The other group consisted of more recent royal dead, including William Rufus; it was possibly at this date that Rufus's body, already disturbed by the collapse of the tower in 1107, was placed in a lead coffer near the high altar.

Bishop Henry's enthusiasm for Roman antiquities and exotic building materials led him to pioneer the use of local decorative stones, especially Purbeck marble. But the font of *c*.1155–65 is of an imported 'marble' from Tournai in modern Belgium. It is the finest of several Tournai fonts which were probably shipped to England in kit form. Two faces of the Winchester font depict miracles of Bishop Nicholas of Myra (Santa Claus), and the detailed view of a ship in one scene is of considerable interest to naval historians, as it includes the earliest depiction of a fixed rudder. These lively images tend to overshadow the other faces, with their Byzantine influenced roundels.

▶ THE MID-12TH-CENTURY TOURNAI MARBLE FONT, WITH SCENES FROM THE LEGEND OF ST NICHOLAS OF MYRA (SANTA CLAUS), MAY HAVE BEEN COMMISSIONED BY BISHOP HENRY OF BLOIS. IT IS THE BEST OF A GROUP OF ENGLISH FONTS WHICH WERE PROBABLY CARVED IN TOURNAI, IN MODERN BELGIUM.

▼ ST NICHOLAS WAS RENOWNED FOR SAVING THE LIVES OF THOSE IN PERIL AT SEA. THE 12TH-CENTURY IMAGE OF A SHIP, WITH ITS HIGH PROW AND FIXED RUDDER, HAS PROVED OF CONSIDERABLE INTEREST TO NAVAL HISTORIANS.

▲ ONE EPISODE DEPICTED ON THE FONT RELATES HOW ST NICHOLAS MIRACULOUSLY BROUGHT THREE STUDENTS BACK TO LIFE AFTER THEY HAD BEEN MURDERED BY AN INNKEEPER.

▲ FROM THE WINCHESTER BIBLE, A DETAIL FROM THE GENESIS INITIAL, SHOWING THE NATIVITY.

▲ From the Winchester Bible, the initial letters to the Gallican and Hebrew versions of Psalm 1, 'Beatus Vir' (the remainder of the opening verse was omitted). They depict David killing a lion and a bear, Christ casting out a demon, and the Harrowing of Hell.

▼ The opening page to II Samuel (II Kings in the Vulgate) from the Winchester Bible. The tall illuminated initial of the word 'Factum' shows the death of King Saul, David's lament, and the killing of the Amalekite.

The Winchester Bible is the supreme product of the cathedral's monastic scriptorium in the time of Bishop Henry, an artistic treasure of world renown. The entire text was copied by a single scribe, but it is the work of the six illuminators which is outstanding, with its exquisite draughtsmanship and lavish use of precious materials: gold leaf and, even more expensive, lapis lazuli, obtainable only from Afghanistan. It is estimated that the skins of over 250 calves were required for its exceptionally large pages. Production must have occupied some 15 years; even so the decoration of the Bible was left unfinished, perhaps following the bishop's death. Nevertheless, it was still possible to use the Bible for its primary purpose: proclaiming the word of God to the monastic community. This priceless artefact is still carried in procession when a new dean or bishop is installed, just as it would have been on important church festivals in the days of St Swithun's Priory.

Also attributed to Bishop Henry is the Holy Sepulchre Chapel, beneath the north tower arch. The Deposition and Entombment scenes on the chapel's east wall are rightly regarded as the finest 12th-century wall paintings in England and are all that survives of its original decoration, which was probably commissioned by Henry of Blois shortly before his death in 1171.

The remaining 12th-century wall paintings in the chapel were destroyed when it was remodelled early in the following century. The original scenes on the east wall survived because they were plastered over to allow a new version to be painted; in 1966 this 13th-century scheme was transferred to the west end of the chapel, revealing the remains of the earlier work. The insertion of the 13th-century vault had destroyed the top of the original painting, but the powerful, Byzantine inspired, image of Christ the Pantocrator (ruler over all) in the vault over the altar compensates for this loss.

▲ THE PAINTING OF CHRIST THE PANTOCRATOR (RULER OVER ALL) ON THE EAST END OF THE VAULT INSERTED INTO THE HOLY SEPULCHRE CHAPEL IN THE EARLY 13TH CENTURY SHOWS THE INFLUENCE OF BYZANTINE ART.

▶ THE 12TH-CENTURY WALL PAINTINGS ON THE EAST WALL OF THE HOLY SEPULCHRE CHAPEL SHOW THE DEPOSITION AND ENTOMBMENT OF CHRIST. THEY WERE PARTIALLY DESTROYED EARLY IN THE 13TH CENTURY WHEN THE CHAPEL WAS VAULTED AND THE EAST WALL WAS REPAINTED, BUT THE ORIGINAL PAINTINGS WERE REVEALED AGAIN IN THE 1960S.

THE LATER MEDIEVAL PERIOD

By the beginning of the 13th century the cathedral was showing its age. Problems with the foundations must have been obvious from the outset, even though Walkelin's builders had tried to create adequate support by using oak piles. The alarming lean of the transept walls shows that they were only partially successful. In 1202 Bishop Godfrey de Lucy, son of Henry II's chief justiciar, inaugurated a 'confraternity for the repair of the church'. The brief went well beyond mere repair, and the east arm was completely remodelled. A new east end was laid out around the Norman work; the design was soon modified so that the central Lady Chapel projected eastwards in a rectilinear version of the Norman scheme. Once the walls had risen above the pavement the Romanesque eastern chapel was demolished, and the work was continued to its full height.

This new work created the retrochoir, a spacious extension providing room for pilgrims to congregate while visiting not only St Swithun's reliquary, still within the apse, but also the relics of St Birinus in the new south-east chapel, and probably other relics besides. As eventually built (some design changes are apparent) it is a 'hall church', with three aisles vaulted at approximately the same height. The impression of spaciousness is reduced by the dominant 15th-century chantry chapels, inserted within the arcades.

▲ BEFORE THE CHANTRY CHAPELS WERE CONSTRUCTED BETWEEN THE ARCADE
PIERS, THE RETROCHOIR WOULD HAVE BEEN AN IMPRESSIVELY OPEN SPACE.

English architecture had progressed considerably since the final years of Henry of Blois, and the retrochoir displays all the features of the new early Gothic style: lancet windows, trefoil wall arcading with quatrefoils in the spandrels, quadripartite vaulting, and the use of Purbeck marble. The somewhat later retrochoir floor, recently cleaned and conserved, is rightly admired as the largest English medieval tile pavement to have survived within a building. It dates from between 1260 and 1280, and the tiles, laid in various configurations in panels separated by plain strips, show a fascinating variety of motifs, despite their worn condition.

But the retrochoir is a pallid reflection of its original appearance, for the survival of red and green pigment in the hollows of the arch mouldings shows that the Caen stonework was originally highly coloured, unlike the Romanesque cathedral, whose decorative effects relied entirely on monumentality. By the 12th century, wall paintings enlivened the transepts; regrettably, two life-sized figures of prophets recorded in 1788 have since disappeared. Important medieval polychromy survives in the Guardian Angels' Chapel, so called after its decoration of large and medium-sized roundels

▶ Bishop Godfrey de Lucy, patron of the construction of the 13th-century retrochoir, was buried in the central nave of the retrochoir, outside the Lady Chapel. Much later, in 1476, the shrine of St Swithun was moved into this part of the cathedral: its position is marked by a memorial dating from 1962.

▲ The Guardian Angels' Chapel is named after the 13th-century decoration of its vault, with its roundels depicting angel heads.

enclosing angel busts. When the vault was first painted (*c*.1220 – 30) these were separated by smaller, plain roundels, but in a later 13th-century repainting the small roundels were replaced by blue backgrounds embellished with attached gilt stars and rosettes.

Bishop de Lucy died in 1204, when the work can only just have begun, and his plain Purbeck marble tomb stands in the centre of his retrochoir. Remains of lead fixings for iron spikes are visible on the lid, which held candles at the annual celebration of his death. Several other important 13th-century monuments lie in the retrochoir, though not in their original positions. The tomb effigy of Peter des Roches (1205 – 38), de Lucy's successor, a statesman-bishop and a crusader, who rode into Jerusalem at the head of an army in 1229, is the earliest in the cathedral: a primitive-looking figure carved in Purbeck marble in low relief.

◀ Recently conserved, the tile pavement of the retrochoir, dating from 1260 – 80, is the largest surviving spread of medieval decorated floor tiles within a building in England.

More accomplished is the heart-burial slab of the infamous Aymer de Valence (1250–60), now located at the end of the north aisle. The body of this unpopular, absentee bishop, half-brother of Henry III, who had forced him on the monks during a personal visit to their Chapter House, was interred in Paris; his heart alone was brought to Winchester.

The other important tomb effigy in the retrochoir is of later date. It portrays Arnaud de Gaveston (died 1302), the only medieval effigy of a layman to survive in the cathedral. He was probably the father of Piers Gaveston, Edward II's much-hated favourite, executed in 1312. Arnaud is portrayed as a knight in chainmail. The supporting tomb-chest is modern; the heraldic front panel of the original chest survives on the east wall of the Guardian Angels' Chapel.

Another tomb-chest, without an effigy, is that of Prior William of Basing (1284–95). It bears the earliest representation in the cathedral of the sword of St Paul and keys of St Peter, which feature in the arms of the see of Winchester. An inscription around the monument states that those who prayed for Prior William's soul would obtain an indulgence – they would be spared so many days in Purgatory.

While these important architectural and artistic treasures were being created, the cathedral continued to feature prominently in English public life. It was in the Chapter House that King John performed his calculated penance before the papal envoys, thus bringing to an end the Pope's embargo on church services known as the Interdict, which must have delayed the completion of the retrochoir. By then the seat of government was at Westminster: the exchequer had moved there during Henry II's reign, and the royal treasury had been transferred there by the late 12th century. No more monarchs were buried in the cathedral after William Rufus.

Nevertheless, some royal events at Winchester should be noted. Richard I ('Lionheart') wore his crown in the cathedral in 1189 and 1194, the latter occasion being effectively a second coronation, watched by his mother, Eleanor of Aquitaine, from a seat on the north side of the choir. Henry III, 'Henry of Winchester', was

▲ Bishop Aymer de Valence (died 1260), an unpopular absentee bishop, was buried in Paris; his heart was brought to Winchester and was buried beneath a slab of Purbeck marble carved with his effigy. The monument was originally near the high altar.

▲ The 'Lillebon panel' of c.1315 was probably the lid of a reliquary chest. An inscription states that it was given to the cathedral by Sir William de Lillebon (Lilbourne, Wiltshire). It is decorated with scenes from the life of Christ, including a charming image of the Virgin and Child.

▲ Winchester's musical tradition goes back to the Middle Ages.
The choristers seen here are the successors of the boys from the
priory's almonry school who sang the daily services in the Lady
Chapel from the 15th century or earlier.

born at Winchester Castle in 1207 and was baptized in the cathedral, possibly in the Tournai marble font. His troubled reign was a difficult period for the monks, who were drawn into the political turbulence when they attempted to resist the king's imposition of foreign bishops. Some monks were imprisoned, and they were even prepared to fight for their political convictions, as they did in 1264 in a brawl with the local citizens over their support for Simon de Montfort. Their resistance to foreign bishops had begun earlier in the century, with the election of Bishop Peter des Roches (1205 – 38). His reputation amongst the Winchester monks as a hard man, a vain and worldly statesman, a foreigner who was more at home in a military camp than a bishop's palace, is softened by a charming tale of how the bishop, lost during a hunting expedition, was invited to the house of an unknown king. It was King Arthur, who, to lend credence to the bishop's story, gave him the power to produce a butterfly from the palm of his hand as a blessing whenever he wished.

The building works, which had faltered to a standstill by around 1230, resumed in the early 14th century. The driving force was Henry Woodlock, born into a gentry family at Marwell, near Winchester. A monk at St Swithun's like his brother, he rose to be prior; on the death of John of Pontoise in 1304 he was elected bishop. Perhaps, having personally experienced life in the monastery, he was particularly sensitive to its needs. Above all, he actually resided in Winchester, unlike several of his predecessors. His episcopate was marked by various building projects, including the monastery guesthouse and the monks' choir stalls. In overall charge of the works was the inspired master mason Thomas of Witney, a craftsman equally adept in stone and timber. At that time the cathedral's eastern arm would have looked sadly unfinished. From his stall a monk with a feel for architectural style would have enjoyed a curious glimpse of the early Gothic retrochoir through the Norman arches at the head of the apse; an original scheme to demolish the apse and link the retrochoir and choir arcades more neatly had been put on hold, and the junction between 'old' and 'new' work must have been very untidy. No doubt this was one of the factors which

▲ An exquisite female statue possibly representing Ecclesia, a personification of the Church, perhaps originally stood in a niche of the surviving 13th-century porch of the prior's house (now the Deanery). The statue is now in the retrochoir.

◀ THE FERETORY SCREEN REPLACED
THE NORMAN APSE IN THE EARLY
14TH CENTURY BUT THE HOLY
HOLE (CENTRE) WAS RETAINED. THE
NICHES FORMERLY HELD STATUETTES
COMMEMORATING THE EARLY
MONARCHS AND BISHOPS WHOSE
REMAINS LAY NEARBY. THESE WERE
DESTROYED AT THE REFORMATION
AND HAVE RECENTLY BEEN REPLACED
BY MODERN ICONS BY THE RUSSIAN
PAINTER SERGEI FYODOROV.

prompted Bishop Woodlock to order the near total replacement of the remaining Norman architecture of the east arm, creating a new presbytery.

Work began *c.*1310, when the Romanesque apse was replaced by two great arches supporting the tall east gable behind the high altar. The arches were supported on a new feretory screen: one of the cathedral's architectural gems and a masterpiece of the Decorated style. This straight screen retained updated versions of several features of the apse which it replaced. Like the apse, it was associated with the cathedral's illustrious dead, lying in their caskets around the high altar. In Henry of Blois's scheme they had been commemorated by inscriptions, fragments of which survive; in the new work the dead kings and bishops were identified by statuettes in niches. They vanished at the Reformation, but their subjects are clear from the names inscribed beneath the empty pedestals. In 1992, the Chapter took the bold decision to place modern icons in the niches, and this exciting work of the Russian icon painter Sergei Fyodorov has brought the feretory screen

back to life as a focus of devotion. The most important feature to be retained in the 14th-century remodelling was the Holy Hole, which was refronted with a pointed arch. Surprisingly, Swithun's relics were not moved into the retrochoir at this stage, for the reliquary can scarcely have been visible from the east.

It was some time before the presbytery was completed. Its original appearance is hard to visualize, because the side arches were filled up by Bishop Fox's openwork stone screens in 1525. Originally the presbytery and its aisles were separated only by low benches, still incorporating the tombs of members of the House of Wessex. The outer walls of the aisles were not rebuilt at this stage, though this must have been the intention. It looks as though the building works were interrupted by the Black Death which reached England in the summer of 1348 and devastated Winchester. The population of the city was halved, not reaching its pre-plague figure again until the mid-19th century.

◄ THE CHOIR WAS REMODELLED IN THE EARLY 14TH CENTURY. THE OAK CHOIR STALLS ARE THOUGHT TO BE THE WORK OF A NORFOLK CRAFTSMAN, WILLIAM OF LYNGWODE.

▲ CHAPELS WERE FORMED IN THE EASTERN AISLES OF THE TRANSEPTS IN THE EARLY 14TH CENTURY. THE CENTRAL CHAPEL IN THE NORTH TRANSEPT RECEIVED A NEW VAULT, SPRINGING FROM DELIGHTFUL CAPITALS, SUCH AS THIS SOMEWHAT DAMAGED SCULPTURE OF AN ANGEL.

Some other small-scale work occurred in the early 14th century, notably in the transepts, where the windows of the eastern aisles were remodelled in Decorated style. They lit chapels in these aisles, replacing simpler altars against the east walls, and the new screens separating the chapels must finally have put paid to the use of the transept aisles as a processional route. Fragmentary wall paintings were still visible on the east wall of the chapels in the south transept in the 19th century, and gave a clue to their dedications.

There was always a pressing need for altar space, even in a cathedral as large as Winchester, for many of the monks would have been in priestly orders and obliged to say personal daily masses, including numerous masses for defunct brethren. Round-headed niches in the east galleries of the transepts probably enclosed altars at this first-floor level: if so, there were 12 altars on the east side of the two transepts. Perhaps altars were also placed against the nave pillars, for William of Wykeham's chantry chapel is said to have been built on the spot where as a boy he had watched the monk Richard Pekis saying his daily mass.

The early 14th-century choir stalls have been called 'the finest set of choir furniture in Europe of their date'. They appear to have been under construction in 1308, when Bishop Henry Woodlock wrote to the Bishop of Norwich asking for a certain 'William of Lyngwode, carpenter' to be excused attendance at his local manorial court until he had completed 'a piece of work belonging to his craft in the choir of our cathedral church'. The letter survives in Woodlock's episcopal register, and is taken as evidence that Lyngwode, who is otherwise unknown, was the master carpenter from Norfolk who designed the choir stalls. They are still used for their original purpose, for it is here that Evensong is sung daily. They now differ greatly from Lyngwode's initial conception. There were originally 64 rear stalls, corresponding to the known number of monks at the time; in front were sub-stalls, most of which have vanished. The seats of the surviving rear stalls are paired, beneath tall, gabled canopies. Each individual stall is separated from its neighbour by a single, thin wooden shaft; the pairs were originally separated by quatrefoil shaft clusters, but these evidently proved

◄ ▲ THE FIGURES IN THE
SPANDRELS BETWEEN THE ARCHES
ABOVE THE REAR SEATS OF WILLIAM
OF LYNGWODE'S CHOIR STALLS ARE
EXQUISITE EXAMPLES OF EARLY
14TH-CENTURY CARVING.

inadequate to support the canopies, and rather crude stanchions were soon introduced. The construction of these stalls was somewhat experimental, and their general design derives from stone architecture.

The decoration of Lyngwode's stalls is rightly admired. The spandrels have lively carvings including human figures: a falconer, whose dress is portrayed in detail, a soldier in chainmail and a surcoat, and a Green Man with sword and shield. In another scene a second Green Man, head thrown back, spews foliage. The animal portraits include a lion trampling its prey, a wyvern, a monkey playing a harp, and a horse standing on a bear-like animal. There may be symbolism here which we no longer fully understand. All these figures inhabit a leafy world, an enchanted forest whose luxuriant trees

and shrubs are recognizable from their foliage, stylized though it is. Wherever possible, tiny human heads adorn the ends of finials and crockets. There are hundreds of them.

Until they fell victim to Puritan iconoclasm, the blank areas above the rear stalls held carved panels with biblical scenes. In 1635 a member of the Noble Military Company in Norwich, Lieutenant Hammond, visited the cathedral and was particularly impressed by these 'lively, wooddy, Representation, Portraicts and Images, from the Creation to the Passion', and listed them in full. On the north side were Old Testament scenes; on the south, episodes from the life of Christ. The panels must have been small-scale, but were evidently of exquisite workmanship. Their loss is an artistic tragedy.

Fortunately the iconoclasts spared the misericords, whose subjects are emphatically secular. These carved ledges beneath the monks' tip-up seats allowed the brethren to perch during the long offices while technically standing. The work is executed with charm and humour: there are human faces in caricature, but also animals (such as the smug cat gripping a dead mouse) and stylized foliage.

Hammond's tally of biblical carvings shows that they continued along the return stalls at the west end of the choir, and we should remember that these stalls originally backed against a stone *pulpitum*: the present openwork screen dates only from *c.*1875. The *pulpitum* was one of two transverse screens separating the 'public' area of the nave from the monks' choir, the other being a rood screen two bays further west. The rood screen, surmounted by an image of Christ Crucified flanked by Saints Mary and John the Evangelist, formed the reredos to the nave altar dedicated to the Holy Cross.

Bishop Woodlock was followed by a succession of prelates who left little mark upon Winchester Cathedral. Rigaud d'Assier was an absentee bishop who was consecrated at St Albans in 1320 and died 30 months later at Avignon; John of Stratford's episcopate lasted ten years before he was translated to Canterbury. Stability returned only in 1345 with the appointment of William of Edington, first of a line of statesman-bishops who occupied the see for the next 200 years.

◀ ▲ MISERICORDS –
LEDGES UNDER THE MONKS'
TIP-UP SEATS – ALLOWED
BRETHREN TO TAKE THE
WEIGHT OFF THEIR FEET
WHILE STANDING DURING
THE LONG SERVICES.

Bishop William of Edington was born *c.*1300 in the Wiltshire village from which he took his name. For a younger son the priesthood provided the best means of advancement, and in 1336 the Bishop of Winchester, Adam of Orleton, recognizing William's talent, appointed him to the living of Chilbolton and to be Master of St Cross Hospital. Edington's career in public service advanced, and by 1344 he was Treasurer of England; he later became Chancellor. At Orleton's death in 1345 the monks tried to elect one of their own number: they still retained a theoretical right to elect their bishop, but royal will frequently prevailed. In this case their decision was overturned by Edward III, who clearly held Edington in high regard; four years later he appointed him first Prelate of the Order of the Garter, a position held by all subsequent bishops of Winchester.

▲ THIS SUPPORTER FROM ONE
OF THE MISERICORDS SHOWS A
SQUIRREL EATING A HAZELNUT.

▶ ANOTHER MISERICORD SHOWS
A CAT HOLDING A DEAD MOUSE.

▶ WILLIAM OF LYNGWODE'S
CHOIR IS STILL USED FOR DAILY
SERVICES, SUCH AS EVENSONG.

Less than 30 months after Edington's consecration the Black Death was ravaging southern England, and his episcopal register records an extraordinary number of ordinations to fill gaps caused by the high mortality amongst clergy. The population of St Swithun's Priory fell from around 60 to 35, and never recovered. Despite these trials, Edington was an enthusiastic building bishop. At Winchester Cathedral he is remembered for initiating the Perpendicular remodelling of the nave, and there is no doubt that he was responsible for the triple porch which replaced the old Norman west front. The porch is an important example of the rapid

◀ THE 14TH-CENTURY WEST FRONT, REPLACING A NORMAN TWIN-TOWERED FAÇADE, WAS BUILT IN TWO PHASES: THE LOWER PART IS THE TRIPLE PORCH OF BISHOP EDINGTON; THE UPPER PART DATES FROM LATER IN THE CENTURY AND WAS DESIGNED BY WILLIAM WYNFORD FOR BISHOP WILLIAM OF WYKEHAM.

▼ THE EARLIEST OF WINCHESTER CATHEDRAL'S OUTSTANDING GROUP OF CHANTRY CHAPELS IS THAT OF BISHOP WILLIAM OF EDINGTON (DIED 1366). HERE DAILY MASSES WERE SAID FOR THE SOUL OF THE DECEASED BISHOP. HIS ALABASTER EFFIGY IS ONE OF THE FINEST MEDIEVAL FIGURE SCULPTURES IN THE CATHEDRAL.

changes in architectural style, from Decorated to Perpendicular, which were perhaps an intentional simplification resulting from the Black Death. Certainly the plague must have delayed Edington's building projects, and his work at Winchester probably consisted of no more than the porch block, erected in an initial stage against the back of the old Norman west front.

Edington was elected Archbishop of Canterbury in 1366 but declined the appointment and died five months later. There seems no truth in the later legend that he claimed 'though Canterbury be the higher rack, yet Winchester is the richer manger'; the generosity of his bequests shows a man who was anything but avaricious. He was succeeded by another royal appointee of even greater renown, William of Wykeham, who entered St Swithun's priory as a novice, rose via Edington's episcopal household to royal service as clerk of works to Edward III at Windsor, was ordained priest at the age of 37, and was elected Bishop of Winchester five years later, in 1366. Like Edington he became Chancellor of England, but as a more lasting memorial he founded New College, Oxford (1379–86) and Winchester College (1382–94), and was patron of the remodelling of the nave of his cathedral.

The work took place in two stages. In a first phase of *c.*1371 only the western façade, together with two bays of the north aisle wall and one of the south, were remodelled. Work was suspended within four years perhaps because of Wykeham's poor relations with the priors of Winchester, but equally owing to the financial and organizational demands of his two educational foundations. Only after his visitation in 1393 were the 'new works' resumed under the inspired direction of the architect William Wynford. In 1845 Professor Willis showed how Wynford skilfully refashioned the Norman elevations into the profiles of the latest Perpendicular architecture, initially by cutting new mouldings into the old stonework and later by recladding the Norman piers and walls. Yet this was emphatically a remodelling rather than a reconstruction: Walkelin's work survives encased within Wynford's refashioning, and Norman masonry may still be seen in the roof spaces.

▲ As patron of the remodelling of the nave, Bishop William of Wykeham was buried in a tall chantry chapel on the south side of his work in 1404.

▶ Recently cleaned and conserved, the stellar lierne vault of the nave was completed in the early 15th century, soon after William of Wykeham's death.

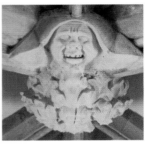

▲ The decorative bosses of the nave vault, including the grotesque heads at the west end, are seen to best advantage through binoculars.

▲ The great west window is a patchwork of fragments of medieval glass, but elements of the original scheme may be made out. The window formed a triptych: scenes from the life of Christ in the central panel were flanked by images of apostles and prophets bearing scrolls with appropriate texts from the Apostles' Creed or the Old Testament.

▶ Fragments of medieval glass which had been recovered after the devastation of the mid-17th century were reassembled in the great west window.

One of Wykeham's last ceremonies in the cathedral was the wedding of Henry IV and Joan of Navarre in February 1403, for he died in September the following year. He was buried in his towering chantry chapel, which is an integral part of the south nave arcade. But the remodelling of the nave was far from complete, as we know from Wykeham's will. The vault was almost all erected after the bishop's death, but his arms, as founder, feature on the bosses throughout its length. The stonework seems never to have been coloured, but stained glass enlivened the new architecture. The great west window is a patchwork reassembled in the 17th century, but fragments of the original triptych-like design are discernible. The central panel showed scenes from the life of Christ; at the sides were images of prophets and apostles bearing scrolls with scriptural texts or sentences of the Apostles' Creed.

Chantry chapels are an important feature of Winchester Cathedral. Edington had already been buried in such a chapel next to the place where the monks assembled to process into the choir. Its modest height suggests that it stood below the Norman main arcade. The purpose of these chapels was to house the altars where masses were said for the souls of the deceased bishops buried within them.

▼ WILLIAM OF WYKEHAM, CHANCELLOR OF ENGLAND AND FOUNDER OF NEW COLLEGE, OXFORD AND WINCHESTER COLLEGE, IS COMMEMORATED BY AN EARLY 15TH-CENTURY ALABASTER TOMB EFFIGY.

MONASTIC LIFE

Our knowledge of life in the cathedral priory, scanty for the early medieval period, increases from the 15th century. The main source comprises over 100 account rolls compiled annually by the obedientiary monks who ran the priory's various departments. They providentially escaped being burnt in the 1860s by a canon intent on cleaning up the cathedral's muniment room, but they are only a tiny remnant of the official records of the priory, many of which perished at the dissolution. Nevertheless, they supplement archaeological discoveries in building up a picture of the priory in the Middle Ages. There are amusing glimpses into daily life, such as the 'boy bishop' ceremony, when one of the almonry boys was elected 'bishop' by his fellows on Holy Innocents' day and had to preach a sermon. He was given an allowance of wine to the value of one shilling, enough for a party with his friends. Another document indicates that monks sometimes kept pet animals: it was the cellarer's responsibility to look after them if through death or disability a monk could no longer do so.

▲ THE CENTRE OF MONASTIC LIFE WAS THE GREAT CLOISTER,
LOCATED ON THE SOUTH SIDE OF THE CATHEDRAL NAVE.

▼ The Chapter House arcade is the oldest fragment of monastic architecture within the Cathedral Close. The monks met daily in the Chapter House, heard a reading from the Rule of St Benedict, and settled the business of the day.

◄ THE DEANERY IS THE SUCCESSOR TO THE MEDIEVAL PRIOR'S HOUSE. THE PORCH WAS BUILT IN THE 13TH CENTURY, AND FORMERLY GAVE ACCESS TO A HALL OF THE SAME DATE. THE PRIOR'S HALL WAS RECONSTRUCTED IN THE MID-15TH CENTURY BUT THE INTERIOR HAS BEEN GREATLY ALTERED.

▲ A 14TH-CENTURY CAPITAL IN THE EAST AISLE OF THE NORTH TRANSEPT REMINDED THE ST SWITHUN'S MONKS OF THE TEMPTATIONS OF THE WORLD OUTSIDE THE PRIORY PRECINCTS. IT SHOWS A LONG-HAIRED YOUNG MAN HOLDING A PAIR OF DICE AND A CHECKERBOARD.

A monk from any other Benedictine monastery being taken on a tour of St Swithun's would have felt instantly at home, for Winchester followed the standard plan with only minor variations. Everything was organized around two cloisters: the Great Cloister alongside the nave, and a Little Cloister further south. The Great Cloister is still discernible; its walls were decorated with blind Norman arcading, which survives, though blocked, for a short length on the east side; the wall against the cathedral was plain. The cloister roof was always a simple lean-to affair, supported on an inner arcade; it never seems to have been subject to Gothic remodelling. On the east side of the cloister was the Chapter House of *c*.1090, whose entrance arcade and side walls survive. This was the priory's assembly place, where a chapter from the Rule of St Benedict was read each morning and the day's business settled. Immediately to the south was the 'dorter' or dormitory, running east-west and raised on an undercroft whose level determines the Dean Garnier Garden now occupying the site. Offset against its south-east corner was the great rere-dorter, the monks' latrine block, served by the cleansing stream called the Lockburn which Bishop Æthelwold had diverted into the precincts of Old Minster. The prior's house, a separate lodging, stood at the south-east corner of the Great Cloister. The surviving parts are the 13th-century porch, with its vaulted ground storey under the prior's chapel, and the 15th-century Prior's Hall, with a magnificent timber roof of *c*.1460.

On the west side of the cloister was the cellarer's range, where the priory's provisions were stored. The undercroft of Number 10 is a surviving portion of these vaulted cellars. On the south side of the cloister stood the refectory, with its associated kitchens and service rooms; these were apparently rebuilt in the 13th century and a few fragments survive in the south-west corner of the cloister. Accounts from the 15th century mention a great crucifix on the east wall of the refectory, said miraculously to have spoken in support of Bishop Æthelwold when he expelled the secular canons, but apart from this we know nothing of what was probably a very large building. We do know, on the other hand, what the monks ate each day during two six-month periods in 1492–3 and 1514–5, thanks to two surviving 'diet rolls'. Thus the monks' Christmas feast in 1492 consisted of onion broth, bread soaked in dripping, loin of venison, beef, spiced vegetables, and eggs; the prior was allowed wine to the cost of one shilling and threepence. This repast should be compared with the monks' Lenten fare on Friday 6 March 1493, comprising minnows as an entrée, salt salmon, mushrooms, and mustard – no doubt a necessary condiment.

The Little Cloister was associated with the infirmary, whose hall stood on the south side. In this important yet self-contained part of the monastery, sick monks were tended and aged ones accommodated, sometimes in private chambers – there was of course no retirement age for a monk, who remained in his monastery until he died. It was in this less private part of the Close that needy people could seek shelter or food. The almonry school was located nearby, from which the cathedral's first boy choristers were recruited.

▲ The carved head of a layman in the Pilgrims' Hall is possibly the portrait of the architect, Thomas of Witney.

◀ The priory guesthouse, known since the 19th century as the Pilgrims' Hall, possesses the earliest surviving hammer-beam roof. It dates from c.1308. The four hammer beams are decorated with carved heads, one of which probably represents the young King Edward II.

▶ Cheyney Court, an Elizabethan timber-framed building just inside the southern entrance to the monastery precincts, served as the bishop's courthouse and now incorporates the porter's lodge.

The best monastic survivals are found in the south-east quarter of the precincts. Here a guesthouse was erected *c.*1308 in which visitors could be accommodated – St Swithun's priory had a deserved reputation for hospitality, a tradition revived today with the creation of the Visitors' Centre. One half of the guesthouse has been restored to something like its original appearance. Now known as the 'Pilgrims' Hall', it boasts the earliest surviving hammer-beam roof. The southern half of the building was the guestmaster's house, now

▲ One of the buildings to survive the dissolution of
St Swithun's Priory was the long range of ten stables, built
just inside the Priory Gate at the end of the 15th century.

incorporated in The Pilgrims' School. Nearby, the long, timber-framed range identified as the priory stables was built *c.*1500, as was the earliest part of Cheyney Court, an enclave of the bishop's domain within the priory precincts. This much-photographed building, with its jettied façade, was the bishop's courthouse, where legal business connected with his area of private jurisdiction, the 'Soke', was transacted.

Other buildings have completely vanished. Contemporary texts mention a great barn, a brewhouse, and a forge; even in its urban location the monastery was self-supporting. The south-west corner of the precincts was the 'Great Garden'; the south-east the prior's garden, with a bridge straddling the extra-mural road to another out-garden, where the monks could walk in contemplation, until this area was appropriated by William of

◀ THE EDUCATION OFFICE ORGANIZES VARIOUS ACTIVITIES FOR SCHOOLCHILDREN TO GAIN AN INSIGHT INTO DAILY LIFE AT ST SWITHUN'S PRIORY. HERE A GROUP OF BOYS LEARN WHAT IT WOULD BE LIKE TO WEAR THE BENEDICTINE MONASTIC HABIT.

Wykeham as part of the site of Winchester College. In the extreme south-east corner of the precincts, Floodstock Mill was powered by the millstream which still flows between the Close and the bishop's palace of Wolvesey.

The monastic timetable followed the *horarium* that St Benedict had originally drawn up in the 6th century, with its round of nine services, beginning with Matins at 2 o' clock in the morning – after which the monks retired to bed again until dawn and the service of Lauds – and ending with Compline. This cycle of daily prayer and intercession, the *Opus Dei*, was the prime purpose of the monastery: to address God on behalf of a flawed humanity. The priory was inherently inward-looking, and the monks' seclusion from the world was symbolized by the high Close wall; what would now be called the 'general public' could gain limited access only to the south-east corner of the precincts and, of course, to the shrine of St Swithun. Thus the cathedral did not exercise a spiritual outreach in the modern sense. Something of the monastic ideal survives at weekday

Evensong, a liturgy combining elements of the monastic offices of Vespers and Compline. Here the men and boys of the choir continue the *Opus Dei* of their Benedictine forebears; the services are attended by sizeable congregations but would be equally valid as an act of worship if there was no congregation at all.

The notion of monastic seclusion should not be pushed too far. True, this was the Benedictine ideal, but the St Swithun's monks could not escape the outside world as their Cistercian cousins sought to do. As we have seen, they were drawn into the political conflicts of the 13th century. The prior was an important personage with social obligations. The monks running the priory's various departments had to visit the estates which provided their income. Ordinary cloister monks would have frequent contact with lay people: at the annual St Giles's Fair, in dealings with numerous priory servants, and with the lay corrodians who, in exchange for a large donation, were permitted to dwell until the end of their days within the priory walls.

THE SIXTEENTH CENTURY

illiam of Wykeham was succeeded by another great statesman, Cardinal Beaufort, Henry IV's half-brother. Three times Chancellor of England, he is remembered as a politician and for his uncompromising attitude towards heretics: he was present at the trial of Joan of Arc, who is commemorated by the statue erected outside the Lady Chapel shortly after her canonization in 1920. Beaufort was the richest man in the kingdom and at his death in 1447 left some of his wealth to his cathedral. As a result the Great Screen was erected behind the high altar; its most admired feature was a silver-gilt panel showing Christ's Passion and Resurrection. Part of the precious metal for this work came from King Edgar's reliquary of St Swithun, melted down after nearly 500 years, for the saint was to have a new shrine. It was to stand in the retrochoir, the old feretory platform being now concealed from the choir. Beaufort also carefully chose the site of his own chantry chapel, alongside the new shrine.

The shrine was inaugurated in 1476, when Swithun's bones were carried around Winchester in an ivory casket, displayed on the high altar during a lengthy service enlivened by choral and instrumental music, and finally placed within the monument. This was of a size implying that the bishop's complete body reposed within it. Yet the attempt at reviving the flagging fortunes of St Swithun's cult, long eclipsed by that of Thomas Becket at Canterbury, never really took off, and pilgrim donations remained disappointingly small. The monks must have wondered whether it was worth retaining the services of the lay shrine-keeper.

The bishop who presided over the inauguration of the new shrine was William of Waynflete, successively headmaster of Winchester College, provost of Eton, and founder of Magdalen College, Oxford. Henry VI had recognized Waynflete's abilities, and on the day of Beaufort's death instructed the St Swithun's monks to elect him. During Waynflete's lifetime the Great Screen

◀ THE EFFIGY OF CARDINAL BEAUFORT IN HIS CHANTRY CHAPEL DATES FROM THE 1660S. HALF-BROTHER TO HENRY IV, HE WAS THE RICHEST MAN IN ENGLAND, AND LEFT PART OF HIS FORTUNE TO THE CATHEDRAL. IT WAS USED IN CONSTRUCTING THE GREAT SCREEN AND RELOCATING THE SHRINE OF ST SWITHUN.

▶ THE MID-15TH-CENTURY CHANTRY CHAPEL OF CARDINAL HENRY BEAUFORT.

▲ THE GREAT SCREEN WAS ERECTED BEHIND THE HIGH ALTAR IN THE
YEARS FOLLOWING CARDINAL BEAUFORT'S DEATH. THE STATUES ARE LATE
19TH-CENTURY REPLACEMENTS. BEHIND THE ALTAR, THE CRIMSON-BOUND
BIBLE AND BOOK OF COMMON PRAYER WERE GIFTS FROM CHARLES II.

was completed and his own chantry chapel was erected in the retrochoir, north of the shrine, matching Beaufort's to the south. Waynflete died at his palace at Bishop's Waltham in 1486, shortly before the birth at Winchester of Prince Arthur, first-born son of King Henry VII, who was baptized in the cathedral. Arthur died in adolescence, and his younger brother Henry inherited the throne, with all the implications that his reign would have for the Church in England.

Within a few years, work began on remodelling the east bay of the Lady Chapel. This bay had already been completely reconstructed in the 14th century, and the make-over of *c.*1500 involved embellishment and the provision of larger windows. It was completed during the time of Priors Hunton (1470–98) and Silkstede (1498–1524), whose rebuses appear within the chapel. The entire chapel was revaulted, and the bosses in the western bay include the arms of Henry VII and Bishop Langton (1493–1501). Scenes in *grisaille* showing miracles of the Virgin were painted on the walls *c.*1510, and ten years later carved stalls were installed: the tradition of fine woodwork had already been revived at Winchester with the panelling and screenwork in Bishop Langton's chantry chapel, formerly the chapel of St Birinus.

▶ SOME ORIGINAL SCULPTURE FROM THE GREAT SCREEN HAS MIRACULOUSLY SURVIVED, INCLUDING A CHARMING MADONNA AND CHILD IN FLEMISH STYLE. THESE IMAGES WERE ORIGINALLY COLOURED.

▲ THE CENTRAL ROUNDEL OF THE EAST BAY OF THE LADY CHAPEL SHOWS THE VIRGIN MARY AS QUEEN OF HEAVEN, SUPPORTED BY ANGELS.

▲ A SECOND ROUNDEL IN THE LADY CHAPEL VAULT DEPICTS GOD THE FATHER WITH HIS HAND RAISED IN BLESSING.

51

▲ THE LADY CHAPEL WAS FIRST BUILT IN THE 13TH CENTURY BUT WAS
EXTENSIVELY REMODELLED IN THE 14TH CENTURY AND C.1500.

The Lady Chapel played an important role in the development of the cathedral's musical tradition. A century earlier John Tyes had been appointed, 'to be of service to the convent by playing the organ and singing at the daily mass of Blessed Mary'. He was also responsible for educating up to four boys in chant. Such were the first small beginnings of the mixed choir of men and boys which survived the Reformation and continues to thrive.

▲ BOSSES FROM THE LADY CHAPEL VAULT (C.1500): A MONKEY COMBS A MAN'S HAIR; A GREEN MAN; A COCKATRICE (OR BASILISK) – A MYTHICAL BEAST COMBINING THE HEAD OF A COCK WITH THE BODY OF A DRAGON; AN OWL.

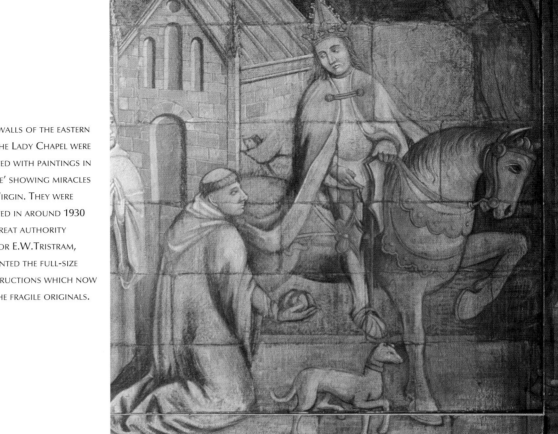

▶ THE WALLS OF THE EASTERN BAY OF THE LADY CHAPEL WERE DECORATED WITH PAINTINGS IN 'GRISAILLE' SHOWING MIRACLES OF THE VIRGIN. THEY WERE CONSERVED IN AROUND 1930 BY THE GREAT AUTHORITY PROFESSOR E.W.TRISTRAM, WHO PAINTED THE FULL-SIZE RECONSTRUCTIONS WHICH NOW COVER THE FRAGILE ORIGINALS.

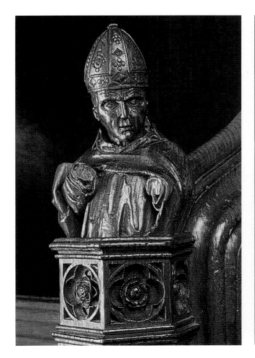

◀ TWO PREACHING FIGURES FROM A SERIES ON THE BUTTRESSES AT THE ENDS OF THE CARVED STALLS (C.1520) OF THE LADY CHAPEL. THESE FIGURES WERE SEVERELY DAMAGED AT THE REFORMATION OR LATER, BUT WERE SKILFULLY RESTORED BY A LOCAL CRAFTSMAN, JAMES THOMAS LAVERTY, IN THE 1890S. THE HEAD OF THE BISHOP AND THE FACE OF THE RIGHT-HAND FIGURE ARE TYPICAL OF HIS WORK.

▼ THE WOODEN VAULT OF THE PRESBYTERY IS AN IMITATION OF THE MUCH EARLIER
NAVE VAULT, AND WAS INSERTED BY BISHOP FOX IN 1503–5. THE HERALDIC BOSSES
WERE ADDED IN 1506. THE CENTRAL BOSS HAS THE INITIALS HR FOR 'HENRICUS REX'
(HENRY VII). BELOW IT APPEAR FOX'S ARMS, INCLUDING THE 'PELICAN IN HER PIETY'.

While work slowly continued on the Lady Chapel, the final major architectural changes were taking place further west, under the patronage of Bishop Fox, Henry VII's Keeper of the Privy Seal and Secretary of State. Thomas Bertie was the architect, and his work shows the first influence of the Renaissance in the cathedral. The presbytery was revaulted between 1503 and 1505, in a wooden version of Wynford's nave vault of a century earlier; in 1506 new bosses were attached to commemorate a visit by the future Henry VIII. From 1506 to 1509 the Romanesque presbytery aisle walls were rebuilt and the aisles were revaulted: plans to remodel the transepts as well were not carried out. Fox's chantry chapel was built between 1513 and 1518. A charming but implausible tradition identifies the chamber at the east end of the chapel as 'Fox's Study', where the bishop, now blind, spent his final days in prayer and meditation. He had retired from state duties in 1516 in order to devote himself to the care of his flock. In 1525 Fox and his steward William Frost paid for openwork stone screens between the 14th-century presbytery arches, and finally new mortuary chests were commissioned to hold the remains of pre-Conquest monarchs and bishops, in an updated version of the arrangements initiated by Henry of Blois. Until the mid-17th century there were eight chests, but only four originals remain, the other two being 17th-century replacements, so further doubling-up of the already jumbled remains occurred, as the Latin inscription on each chest makes clear. By a strange twist of fate, the bones of Queen Emma now lie entangled with those of Bishop Ælfwyn: the pair had been charged with an adulterous relationship during their lifetime, but Emma proved her innocence by means of the 'ordeal by fire', walking on nine red-hot ploughshares.

As events inexorably led towards its dissolution, St Swithun's Priory was anything but moribund.

Indeed, a slight increase in the number of monastic professions may be discernible in the early 16th century, as at other cathedral priories. St Swithun's continued to send two of its brethren to be educated at Oxford. Several building projects are recorded: the monastery stables were erected just inside the south entrance to the precincts, and the upper storey of the porch of the prior's house was altered and re-roofed: the prior's chapel moved elsewhere and an audit house was established where revenues from the monastic estates could be accounted for. So late as 1533 the infirmary hall was re-roofed and its windows reglazed, and major repairs took place in the retrochoir. Everything suggests a monastery in full vigour.

▶ THE CORBELS SUPPORTING THE PRESBYTERY VAULT TAKE THE FORM OF ANGELS HOLDING SHIELDS BEARING THE ARMS OF THE SEE OF WINCHESTER AND OF BISHOP FOX; ALSO THE INSTRUMENTS OF CHRIST'S PASSION.

◀ IN 1525 BISHOP FOX AND HIS STEWARD, WILLIAM FROST, BUILT STONE SCREENS BETWEEN THE PIERS OF THE PRESBYTERY. THEY SUPPORT RENAISSANCE MORTUARY CHESTS CONTAINING THE BONES OF PRE-CONQUEST MONARCHS AND BISHOPS WHICH HAD LONG BEEN LOCATED NEAR THE HIGH ALTAR.

▶ THE FINAL SHRINE OF ST SWITHUN WAS DESTROYED IN 1538. SINCE 1962 THE SITE OF THE SHRINE HAS BEEN MARKED BY A MODERN MEMORIAL.

Nevertheless, in 1535 and again in 1536 the king's commissioners, including Thomas Cromwell in person, descended on Winchester. In March 1536 Prior Henry Brooke was replaced by William Basing, a member of an extensive Hampshire family and viewed as potentially 'conformable' with the anticipated changes. The dissolution was heralded by the destruction of St Swithun's shrine during the night of 21–22 September 1538. The avaricious commissioner, Thomas Wriothesley, expressed disappointment that 'there was no gold, nor ring, nor true stone in it, but all great counterfeits'; the value of the silver (£1,333) was some consolation. The fate of Swithun's bones is not known, though a contemporary account recorded that they were 'laid safe'. But his skull, taken to Canterbury by St Alphege *c.*1005, had found its way to Évreux in Normandy by the 14th century, where it still resides in the cathedral treasury. Other Winchester relics were smuggled abroad at the Reformation, such as the reputed foot of St Philip, which one of the monks, Thomas Figg, saved from a pile of relics destined for the bonfire, and took with him to St Andrew's monastery, Bruges.

The priory formally surrendered to the king on 14 November 1539. During an 18-month hiatus the cathedral's valuables were appropriated and the new cathedral statutes were drawn up. Prior Basing became

▲ The initial letter to the Letters Patent granting former estates of the Priory of St Swithun to the new Dean and Chapter shows Henry VIII handing the document to William Kingsmill, last Prior of St Swithun's and first Dean of Winchester.

the new dean, reverting to his family name of King-smill, and the present Dean of Winchester is therefore the direct successor of a line of priors going back to the 10th century. Offices were found for several of the more competent monks; it is difficult, however, to chart these changes, for like Basing they reverted to their family names on shedding the monastic habit. The cathedral was now to be run by a dean and 12 canons (called preb-endaries), together with 12 minor canons; these clerics were supported by lay officers specified in the founda-tion statutes, including sub-sacrists, virgers, bellringers, singing men, and choristers. The communal property of the monastic close was divided up: each canon would maintain a separate household. For the other members of the foundation a 'Common Table' was established in the old prior's hall (the statutes provided for a manciple, two cooks, and two butlers).

The dissolution left its mark on the Cathedral Close. The refectory and dormitory were early casualties, being deemed 'superfluous'; their lead roofs were estimated for sale. The infirmary hall lasted somewhat longer. Many of the other buildings around the cloisters could be turned into accommodation for the canons.

Within the cathedral, the Holy Hole was stopped up and the statuary removed from the Great Screen. The torsos of the statues provided useful building material for the walls required between the canons' private gar-dens; the heads were probably buried in the infill behind the Great Screen. The high altar was removed, eventually to be replaced by a wooden table, and the Ten Com-mandments were painted on a board behind it in place of Beaufort's silver-gilt altar panel. Additional choir stalls were commissioned, whose panels included the arms of Dean Kingsmill, the royal arms, and the new arms granted to the Dean and Chapter on 1 June 1541.

Changes to the style of worship were introduced during Edward VI's short reign, notably the introduc-tion of the first Book of Common Prayer in 1549, before Queen Mary's accession brought about a brief return to Catholicism. Bishop Stephen Gardiner was reinstated in August 1553 after five years' imprisonment in the Tower of London. On 25 July the following year he presided at a major event in the cathedral, Mary's wedding to Philip

◀ THE STATUARY OF THE GREAT SCREEN WAS PULLED DOWN AT THE REFORMATION. THE TORSOS WERE USED IN NEW WALLS WITHIN THE CLOSE, BUT THE HEADS WERE HIDDEN, PERHAPS BEHIND THE SCREEN ITSELF. THE HEAD OF GOD THE FATHER, WEARING THE PAPAL TIARA, WOULD HAVE BEEN AN OBVIOUS TARGET FOR THE ICONOCLASTS.

▼ THE REALISTIC HEADS OF BISHOPS WERE PROBABLY MODELLED FROM LIFE AND WERE ORIGINALLY COLOURED. THE STATUARY OF THE GREAT SCREEN WAS REPLACED AT THE END OF THE 19TH CENTURY.

of Spain. Lively accounts of proceedings have survived by three of Philip's courtiers, refreshed after their three-day summer cruise from La Coruña: the Spanish party stayed at the Deanery, while Mary was accommodated at Wolvesey Palace to avoid sleeping under the same roof as her fiancé until they were married. The cathedral nave was hung with Flemish tapestries for the occasion, showing victories of Philip's father, Charles V, over the 'infidel' at Tunis; they were subsequently taken back to Spain. The wedding was celebrated by a magnificent banquet and a ball at Wolvesey, where language difficulties impeded relations between the Spanish nobles and the English ladies. The Spanish contingent found time for a tour of the cathedral, pronouncing it 'one of the most beautiful temples ever seen', and did some sightseeing in town, where they admired the Round Table.

Gardiner lived 16 months more, but his health was failing, and he died at Southwark in November 1555. Poor roads prevented his body from being transported to Winchester until late February, when it was placed in a temporary brick structure north of the high altar while his chapel was constructed. The bishop had left

◄ A 16TH-CENTURY X-FRAME CHAIR, NOW DISPLAYED IN THE TRIFORIUM GALLERY, HAS LONG BEEN CLAIMED AS THE SEAT USED BY MARY TUDOR AT THE TIME OF HER MARRIAGE TO PHILIP OF SPAIN IN 1554. IT WAS SMASHED BY THE PARLIAMENTARIANS IN 1642 BUT WAS REPAIRED AT THE RESTORATION OF THE MONARCHY (1660).

▲ FOR THE WEDDING OF MARY TUDOR TO PHILIP OF SPAIN THE NAVE WAS HUNG WITH TAPESTRIES. TODAY, BATIK BANNERS DESIGNED BY THETIS BLACKER ILLUSTRATING THE CREATION ADORN THE NAVE DURING MAJOR FESTIVALS: THIS ONE DEPICTS THE 'MAIESTAS', A VISION OF GOD ENTHRONED IN HEAVEN.

▲ The monastic dormitory was no longer required after the
Dissolution, and became part of the Dean's garden. The garden created
on this site by Dean Thomas Garnier (1840–72) has recently been restored,
and provides a haven of quiet for visitors to the Cathedral Close.

money for a chantry even though technically these had been illegal since 1547. The chapel is a magnificent hybrid: a Gothic carcase decorated in the High Renaissance idiom of Fontainebleau.

The Catholic revival under Mary had little effect on the architecture and furnishings of the cathedral. In 1571, after the return to Protestantism, Bishop Horne held a visitation and directed that the rood loft should be walled up. Other vestiges of the cathedral's monastic past were obliterated. The infirmary hall had been demolished in 1570: the Chapter House survived until 1580, after which chapter meetings were held on the upper floor of the old rood loft. The priory guesthouse (the Pilgrims' Hall) was spared by being adapted as the Dean and Chapter's common brewhouse: beer was an essential beverage in days when it was unsafe to drink water, even though the Close still enjoyed the benefit of a piped water supply, a relic of monastic days.

THE SEVENTEENTH CENTURY

The history of Winchester Cathedral in the 17th century is dominated by the Commonwealth and its aftermath, but various changes to the fabric occurred before the Civil War. An unusually personal insight is provided by the diary of John Young, Dean of Winchester during those increasingly turbulent years, from 1616 to 1645, when he was exiled to Nether Wallop, where he died nine years later.

The opening entries in Young's Winchester diary mention repairs to the cathedral, which were apparently much needed, though funding was a problem and a begging letter to the Chapter's tenants proved ineffectual. Not all the works involved alterations to the fabric: one of Young's first actions was to 'remove the sermons' to the nave; the choir he considered cramped, 'pushed with ill-fashioned pews'. Various projects took place in the tower. Originally this had been an open 'lantern', but by the mid-16th century, possibly earlier still, a bell chamber and ringing chamber had

▶ THE LONG GALLERY WAS ADDED TO THE REBUILT DEANERY IN 1673, PERHAPS SO THAT THE DEAN COULD RECEIVE CHARLES II IN APPROPRIATE STATE.

▲ SMALL STATUES REPRESENTING THE STUART KINGS ORIGINALLY STOOD AT THE CORNERS OF THE TOWER VAULT. THEY WERE REMOVED IN 1819.

◀ THE WOODEN TOWER VAULT IMITATES THE EARLIER VAULTING OF THE NAVE AND PRESBYTERY. THE CENTRAL ROUNDEL, RESTORED TO ITS ORIGINAL APPEARANCE IN 1992, IS A REMOVABLE BELL-TRAP; AROUND THE EDGE, THE RED LETTERS ARE A 'CHRONOGRAM' AND MAY BE REORDERED INTO THE DATE MDCXXXV: 1635.

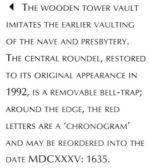

been inserted. The bells were rehung in a new frame in the 1630s. Its 18th-century replacement is still in use and may incorporate timbers from the earlier frame. The ringing chamber floor must have been deemed unsightly, and in the mid-1630s a wooden ceiling vault was constructed with tracery echoing the medieval vaults on either side. It originally sprang from four corner corbels crudely representing the Stuart kings; these were likened in 1819 to 'Scotchmen playing their bagpipes' and were removed. The vault has recently been restored to its original colour scheme, and the central roundel (a removable bell-trap) has reverted to its first design showing a sunburst, representing God, and three groups of angels, together with the Hebrew words 'Holy, Holy, Holy', a typical Laudian conceit.

The tower vault bosses include, as well as heraldry, a roundel portraying Charles I and Henrietta Maria. A year or so later the king visited the cathedral, where he was unimpressed by the 'chapter house' (the old rood loft), claiming that it projected too far into the nave. The Dean and Chapter took this to heart, and by 1636 Inigo Jones had been commissioned to produce a new choir screen in Classical style, completed within four years. It included niches with life-size statues of Charles I and James I by Herbert Le Sueur, now relocated at the west end of the nave. Other innovations included Laudian altar rails to enclose the sanctuary, and a canopy over the high altar (which is now displayed in the Triforium Gallery).

▲ STATUES OF CHARLES I AND JAMES I – SHOWN HERE – WERE COMMISSIONED FROM THE SCULPTOR HERBERT LE SUEUR TO STAND IN NICHES IN THE INIGO JONES CHOIR SCREEN OF C.1636. DURING THE PERIOD OF PARLIAMENTARY RULE THEY WERE HIDDEN IN THE ISLE OF WIGHT. THEY WERE REUSED IN A GOTHIC CHOIR SCREEN OF 1820 – 4 BUT NOW STAND AT THE WEST END OF THE NAVE.

◀ AMONGST THE BOSSES OF THE TOWER VAULT IS A PORTRAIT OF KING CHARLES I AND HIS QUEEN, HENRIETTA MARIA.

In all these works, John Young was fully supported by his bishops. After the Reformation a new class of prelate had emerged. They were spiritual leaders, usually with university backgrounds, rather than the statesmen who had been awarded bishoprics as a result of their rise to political power. One such new bishop was Lancelot Andrewes, elected in 1618 and still remembered with affection in Winchester. He played a prominent part in establishing the young Church of England, and was one of the translators of the Authorized Version of the Bible and author of the devotional work *Private Prayers*. In 1632 Walter Curle was enthroned, a churchman in the Laudian mould. Like his dean, he was concerned with making the cathedral a more reverent place of worship. When in 1635 the cathedral was officially visited by the Vicar-General, Sir Nathaniel Brent, before new Cathedral Statutes were issued in 1637, one concern was that the nave served as a thoroughfare, even though shortly after his translation to Winchester Bishop Walter had created 'Curle's Passage' around the south-west corner of the cathedral; an ingenious Latin anagram and a pointing hand on the west front still direct passers-by to this short cut.

John Young was dean during a period of increasing political tension. One symptom was a dispute with the city's mayor and corporation over the payment of 'ship-money', a tax levied to support the Fleet. The Chapter had already contributed a lump sum to the High Sheriff's official (and had a receipt to prove it), so they protested to the king when the city corporation made a second demand and two of the cathedral's employees were imprisoned for non-payment. The debate rumbled on for several years. Meanwhile relations with the city deteriorated to the point of farce: the canons complained when the mayor and corporation bore their maces when attending cathedral services, claiming that the Close lay outside city jurisdiction. The corporation paid little regard to a royal instruction against the carrying of these 'ensigns of authority'; on receiving the royal command the mayor shoved it into his pocket and twice entered the cathedral, his hat on his head, preceded by an official carrying his mace. A further argument ensued over where the mayor should sit in the choir.

▲ THE WOODEN BELL FRAME DATES FROM THE 18TH CENTURY, BUT INCORPORATES TIMBERS FROM AN EARLIER, POSSIBLY 17TH-CENTURY, FRAME. FURTHER BELLS HAVE BEEN ADDED MORE RECENTLY.

▲ THE MEMORIAL TO LANCELOT ANDREWES, ELECTED BISHOP OF WINCHESTER IN 1618, IS THE WORK OF THE MODERN SCULPTOR, SIMON VERITY. ANDREWES WAS ONE OF THE TRANSLATORS OF THE AUTHORIZED VERSION OF THE BIBLE AND AN INFLUENTIAL FIGURE IN THE CHURCH OF ENGLAND DURING ITS FORMATIVE YEARS.

▲ Modern misericords showing the 'Pelican in her Piety' and a lion and his cubs, carved by the Sussex-born artist Susan Wraight in 1988–9 to replace missing originals which were probably destroyed by Parliamentarian troops in 1642.

These irritations were quickly overshadowed when in August 1642 Winchester Castle surrendered to the Parliamentarian leader Sir William Waller. He had little control over his troops, who, disgruntled at not being paid, took to looting. Their activities were vividly described by the Royalist pamphleteer Bruno Ryves, later Dean of Windsor. On 13 December the soldiers broke open the west doors of the cathedral and marched up the aisle 'with Colours flying, their drums beating, their Matches fired'. Some rode their horses through the church. Their worst destruction was reserved for the choir, where they smashed the carved panels with their Old and New Testament scenes, and pulled down the mortuary chests, using the bones of Saxon kings and bishops as missiles with which to break the windows. Then some of the troopers donned surplices and other vestments and rode through the streets of Winchester bearing organ pipes, prayer books, and fragments from the 14th-century choir stalls.

Such was the melancholy prelude to the Commonwealth. The dean and canons were ejected in 1645. Four years later an official survey was made of the Close buildings; it is an essential document for understanding the layout of the canonry houses between the Reformation and the Civil War. These houses were shared out amongst Parliamentary supporters, and many were demolished for their building materials. Services ceased in the cathedral, unsuitable for worship in the eyes of Puritan ministers, and its very fabric was threatened. In the 1650s a group of citizens drew up a petition begging for the cathedral to be spared demolition: it was a 'most convenient and spatious place of assemblinge for the hearinge of God's word'.

One man is recalled with gratitude for the part he played during these troubles. John Chase, the chapter clerk, retrieved several of the cathedral's documents after the cathedral muniment room was ransacked in 1642 and again in 1646. He recorded how 'divers large parchments they made kytes withall to flie in the ayre'; one medieval document was 'given me by Tupper the butcher all soyled and found by him in Winchester High Street'.

In 1660 the canons returned to a devastated Close. Of the Deanery and 12 canonry houses, only three houses survived unscathed, and two in part, the others having been demolished. The Chapter's first income from new leases was devoted to rebuilding the Close, and the opportunity was taken of distributing the canons' houses more evenly. The new works included the interesting group of four brick houses in Dome Alley, formerly a garden area. The Deanery was rebuilt: at first a modest dwelling, whose main rooms were formed by inserting a floor and crosswalls into the medieval Prior's Hall, it was enlarged *c.*1673 with the addition of the Long Gallery, where the dean could receive Charles II in appropriate state during the king's visits to the city which he hoped to make a kind of English Versailles. One person who was not welcome in the Deanery was Charles's mistress, Nell Gwyn; Canon Thomas Ken (later Bishop of Bath and Wells and a famous hymn writer) then refused to allow her to occupy his canonry house, which stood near to the Deanery. Eventually accommodation was found at the south end of the Prior's Hall, where a brick building called 'Nell Gwyn' was demolished only in 1808.

Damage in the cathedral was not as severe as it might have been. The choir stalls were repaired and the pinnacles above their canopies were gilded. The statues of Charles I and James I were reinstated: they had been taken to the Isle of Wight, where they were bought by a Royalist sympathizer, who buried them in his garden. A contract was drawn up in 1665 with Thomas Thamer for a new 'faire, substantial good and perfect double Organ', and ten years later the bells were recast. A new altar rail was provided.

The bishop during this period of reconstruction was George Morley (1662–84), a man of deep personal holiness and wide learning. His benefactions included Morley College, a group of dwellings on the edge of the churchyard for clergy widows, and the collection of about 2,000 books which he left for the use of canons and diocesan clergy, together with bookshelves to accommodate them. The cathedral had possessed a library since the Laudian reforms; in the 1680s it

◀ THOMAS THAMER'S ORGAN WAS DECORATED WITH ANGELS POSSESSING ARTICULATED ARMS WHICH ALLOWED THE ORGANIST TO CONDUCT THE CHOIR WHILE ACCOMPANYING THE SINGERS ON THE ORGAN.

▼ A HERALDIC UNICORN FROM THE ORGAN CASE OF 1665 BY THOMAS THAMER.

was relocated over the slype at the end of the south transept, in rooms once used as the monastic sacrist's offices. The library has scarcely changed since Morley's day, and is used regularly by scholars.

Bishop Morley's steward at Farnham Castle, where he resided until Wolvesey Palace was rebuilt, was Izaak Walton, renowned in his day as a biographer but now popularly remembered for *The Compleat Angler*. During his final years he lived in Number 7, The Close with his son-in-law, Canon Hawkins; after his death in 1683 the probate inventory of his belongings itemized 'Fishing Tackle and other lumber'.

▶ THE CHAPEL OF ST JOHN THE EVANGELIST AND THE FISHERMEN APOSTLES CONTAINS THE GRAVE OF IZAAK WALTON AND IS A PLACE OF PILGRIMAGE FOR ANGLERS. THE MODERN ALTAR FURNITURE IS THE WORK OF PETER EUGENE BALL.

◀ AT HIS DEATH IN 1684 BISHOP GEORGE MORLEY BEQUEATHED TO THE DEAN AND CHAPTER HIS COLLECTION OF ABOUT 2,000 BOOKS, TOGETHER WITH SHELVES (C.1635), SAID TO COME FROM FARNHAM CASTLE. HE ALSO GAVE £50 FOR TWO GLOBES, 'TO BE PLACED IN THE UPPER END OF THE LIBRARY': THE TERRESTRIAL AND CELESTIAL GLOBES ARE THE WORK OF WILLEM JANSZOON BLAEUW.

▶ THE EAST WINDOW OF THE CHAPEL WAS PAID FOR IN 1914 BY 'THE FISHERMEN OF ENGLAND AND AMERICA'. IT INCLUDES A PORTRAIT OF IZAAK WALTON, SITTING BY THE RIVER ITCHEN.

THE EIGHTEENTH AND NINETEENTH CENTURIES

The life of the cathedral in the 18th century is usually regarded as introspective, somnolent, and devoid of incident. The words of Canon Pyle (1756–76) are often cited: 'The life of a prebendary is a pretty easy way of dawdling away one's time: praying, walking, visiting; and as little study as your heart would wish.' More objective were the comments of writers visiting the cathedral: almost all noted the small congregations, and the comfort and wealth of its clergy. Dean Cheyney (1748–60) was remembered less as a churchman than as an astute financier who gave a huge party at the Deanery in 1756 – and for the splendour of his funeral. To his credit, he donated two candelabra, one of which hangs before the high altar, and earned the gratitude of Jean Serres, a Huguenot whose Latin memorial in the Epiphany Chapel tells a gripping tale of a man who never abandoned his Protestant principles, despite 27 years as a slave in galleys operating from Marseilles.

This was a lethargic period in the life of the cathedral – indeed for the Church – and work to the fabric may be simply summarized. Urns were placed in the empty niches of the Great Screen in 1700; a new throne was erected for Bishop Trelawney (1707–21); the bell frame was extended in 1734; the pavement of the choir and presbytery was relaid in 1764. A painting by Benjamin West depicting the Raising of Lazarus was placed above the high altar in 1781, in the space once occupied by Cardinal Beaufort's altar panel.

This lack of activity in the cathedral church was in some measure counterbalanced by the lives and works of a few individual bishops and canons who managed to escape the general torpor. The absentee Bishop Hoadly (1734–61) visited his cathedral just once, in 1736 – like many of his contemporaries, he was enthroned by proxy – but he had achieved renown while previously Bishop of Bangor (which he probably never visited) through his outspoken writings on church authority, the so-called 'Bangorian Controversy'. Equally controversial were the views of Dean Shipley (1760–9), a radical, and a friend of Benjamin Franklin, whom he entertained at his home at Twyford near Winchester: he keenly supported American independence, later describing North America as 'the only great nursery of freemen left on the face of the earth'.

Prebendary William Lowth (1696–1732) also stood out as a scholar and conscientious pastor. A Hebrew specialist, he wrote extensively on the Old Testament. Even more distinguished was his son, Archdeacon Robert Lowth, who first developed the concept of 'parallelism' in Hebrew poetry, and published an important biography of William of Wykeham. Dean Zachary Pearce (1739–48), later appointed Bishop of Rochester, was also highly regarded for his scholarship in the field of classical literature and New Testament studies.

On the altar frontal: *He shall ✠ save his ✠ people from ✠ their sins*

◀ JOHN FLAXMAN'S CHARMING MEMORIAL TO JOSEPH WARTON (1722–1800) COMMEMORATES A WELL-LOVED HEADMASTER OF WINCHESTER COLLEGE AND CANON OF THE CATHEDRAL, WHERE HE LIES BURIED IN THE NORTH AISLE. HE IS SHOWN INSTRUCTING FOUR PUPILS WHILE ARISTOTLE AND HOMER PRESIDE IMPASSIVELY.

▲ THE ALTAR-PIECE BY CHARLES EAMER KEMPE IN THE LADY CHAPEL, SHOWING THE ANNUNCIATION, COMMEMORATES THE CHRISTIAN WRITER CHARLOTTE YONGE (1823–1901) AND WAS GIVEN IN 1905 BY HER FRIENDS AND ADMIRERS OF HER BOOKS.

Other canons were notable for public works and philanthropy. Alured Clarke founded the County Hospital in Winchester and made provision for the continuing financial support of its poorer patients.

Towards the end of the century, the Dean and Chapter turned their attention once more to the maintenance and embellishment of their great cathedral, described by one visitor as 'a scene of general devastation'. In 1775 the architect James Essex surveyed the building, followed by the notorious James Wyatt, whose restoration works at Salisbury and Lincoln earned him the nickname 'the Destroyer'; fortunately his operations at Winchester were restricted to modest repairs. Then in 1809 the Chapter appointed their first architectural surveyor, William Garbett, who was concerned at the evident subsidence of many of the cathedral's walls, and the state of two pillars flanking Bishop Edington's chantry chapel. His suggested remedy was queried by the Chapter, who sought a second opinion from John Nash: the piers were reinforced with cast-iron shafts, ingeniously sheathed in artificial stone.

The most important influence on the fabric of the cathedral during this period was Prebendary George Frederick Nott, who combined scholarship with a passion for architecture which found practical expression at Winchester, where he was supported by Dean Thomas Rennell. He personally supervised the repairs, and was undaunted by a fall from a ladder in 1816: during his lengthy convalescence in Italy he translated the Book of Common Prayer into Italian. In 1820–4 the Inigo Jones choir screen was replaced by a Gothic screen, designed by William Garbett in imitation of Edington's west porch. Disagreement within the Chapter as to whether the organ should be relocated on the new screen rumbled on for several years. Meanwhile the flat ceilings in the transepts were installed to Nott's own design. Prebendary Nott was also responsible for reordering many of the cathedral's medieval monuments, to the confusion of later historians.

In recent years one tomb in Winchester Cathedral has attracted more attention than any other. It is that of Jane Austen, who lodged in nearby College Street for the final weeks of her life in order to be closer to her physician,

dying there on 18 July 1817. She is one of several famous local women associated with the cathedral, including Charlotte Yonge, the writer; Josephine Butler, the social campaigner; and Mary Sumner, founder of the Mothers' Union, who lived at Number 1, The Close with her husband George Sumner, Archdeacon of Winchester and, later, suffragan Bishop of Guildford.

In 1835 – 6 the Cathedrals Act brought about wide-ranging changes in cathedral and Close. Within a few years the number of canons began to be reduced from twelve to five, and two of the canonry houses in the Close were demolished. Others later found a new use:

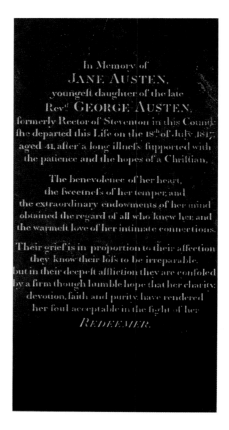

▲ THE TOMB SLAB OF JANE AUSTEN (1775–1817) DOES NOT MENTION HER LITERARY ACHIEVEMENTS, BUT A MEMORIAL BRASS WAS ADDED NEARBY IN 1872. IN 1900 A MEMORIAL WINDOW BY C.E. KEMPE WAS ERECTED ABOVE THE GRAVE BY PUBLIC SUBSCRIPTION.

▶ THE PRESENT ORGAN CASE WAS DESIGNED BY EDWARD BLORE IN 1824 AND WAS LATER ADAPTED TO HOLD A LARGE PART OF THE ORGAN THAT 'FATHER' HENRY WILLIS HAD ORIGINALLY BUILT FOR THE GREAT EXHIBITION OF 1851. A SECOND ORGAN CASE, HOUSING A NAVE ORGAN, WAS ADDED IN 1987.

▲ THE WILBERFORCE MEMORIAL, COMPLETED IN 1878, IS DECORATED
WITH CHARMING EXAMPLES OF VICTORIAN SCULPTURE.

Number 4 has served as the Judges' Lodgings since 1897; Number 3 is The Pilgrims' School; and other houses have been adapted for use as offices or accommodation for the cathedral staff.

The cathedral's musical tradition gradually recovered during the 19th century. True, some interesting individual musicians may be noted in the previous centuries: the composer Adrian Batten, a Winchester chorister who later carved his name on the stonework of the Gardiner chantry chapel; the organist John Reading, who was reprimanded for beating his choristers over-severely and wrote the Winchester school song *Dulce Domum*; Charles Dibdin, another chorister, whose solo recitals earned him fame at the Winchester races and concert rooms, and who in later life composed *Tom Bowling* in memory of his brother, who had been killed by lightning at the Cape of Good Hope. But musical standards were dire and the cathedral's organists of poor musical calibre – such as Dr Chard, who, as the canons complained in 1818, 'attended at the singing room only 14 times, having been once absent for more than 3 months altogether', and found hunting more congenial than harmony. Things could only change for the better when Samuel Sebastian Wesley was appointed organist in 1849. He played an important role in the 19th-century revival of interest in church music, as organist and composer, and he persuaded the Dean and Chapter to buy two-thirds of the huge organ which 'Father' Willis had built for the Great Exhibition of 1851.

Two of the cathedral's architectural features were changed later in the 19th century. In 1874 it was proposed to replace William Garbett's Gothic choir screen by the present openwork screen designed by Sir George Gilbert Scott, as a memorial both to Bishop Wilberforce ('Soapy Sam', whose cenotaph is an inescapable feature of the south transept) and to Dean Garnier. Then in 1884 an appeal was launched to repopulate the niches of the Great Screen in memory of Archdeacon Philip Jacob, a popular local figure. The choice of statuary proved controversial, and the completion of the project was further delayed by arguments over the central representation of Christ Crucified. The new work was finally dedicated in 1899.

◀ THE MEMORIAL TO BISHOP
SAMUEL WILBERFORCE (DIED
1873), AFTER A DESIGN BY
SCOTT, DOMINATES THE SOUTH
TRANSEPT. THE SON OF THE
SOCIAL REFORMER, WILBERFORCE
WAS BISHOP OF OXFORD, THEN
OF WINCHESTER, AND WAS GIVEN
THE NICKNAME 'SOAPY SAM' BY
HIS OPPONENTS IN THE POLITICAL
DEBATES OF THE DAY.

THE TWENTIETH CENTURY AND THE NEW MILLENNIUM

The early years of the 20th century were dominated by the great preservation works of 1905–12, intended to deal once and for all with the problems of subsidence by underpinning the medieval walls on new concrete foundations. These had to descend 4 metres (13 feet) below the water table, and progress was slow until the consultant engineer, Francis Fox, realized that a diver could achieve the desired result without the need for pumping out the excavations. William Walker, the diver, is commemorated annually at Winchester's Patronal Festival as the man who 'saved the cathedral with his own hands'.

▲ A ROUNDEL BY ERIC GILL IN THE EPIPHANY CHAPEL SHOWING THE 'AGNUS DEI' (LAMB OF GOD), PURCHASED BY THE CATHEDRAL IN 1993.

▶ THE STATUE OF JOAN OF ARC, CARVED UNDER THE SUPERVISION OF SIR NINIAN COMPER, WAS DEDICATED IN 1923, THREE YEARS AFTER HER CANONIZATION. IT WAS GIVEN BY A GROUP OF ENGLISH AND AMERICAN PEOPLE WHO FELT THAT THE DIOCESE SHOULD MAKE SOME REPARATION FOR CARDINAL BEAUFORT'S INVOLVEMENT IN HER TRIAL.

▼ THE EPIPHANY CHAPEL WAS CREATED IN THE WESTERN AISLE OF THE
NORTH TRANSEPT UNDER THE DIRECTION OF CANON ARTHUR SUTTON
VALPY, WHO PAID FOR THE WORK BUT DIED IN 1909 BEFORE THE CHAPEL
WAS COMPLETED; THE WINDOWS WERE DEDICATED IN HIS MEMORY.

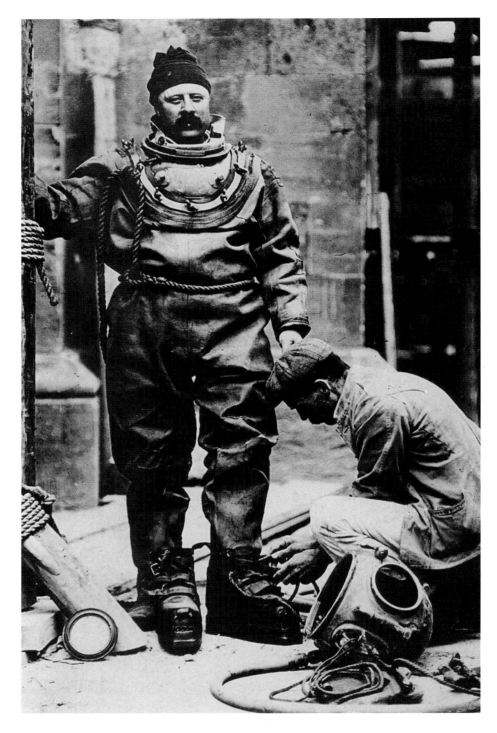

◀ WILLIAM WALKER, A DEEP-SEA
DIVER, TOILED BELOW THE WALLS
OF THE CATHEDRAL FOR NEARLY
SIX YEARS (1906–11) IN ORDER
TO REPLACE THE FOUNDATIONS.

▶ THE BUTTRESSES ON THE
SOUTH SIDE OF THE NAVE WERE
ADDED IN 1911–2.

Although the involvement of a diver captured the public's imagination, Walker was in fact only a key member of a team of about 150 workmen who, over a six-year period, laboured on a complete preservation operation, directed by the famous architect Thomas Jackson. The final phase of the work involved the addition of buttresses along the south side of the cathedral. The completion of the works was celebrated by a Service of National Thanksgiving on St Swithun's Day 1912, attended by King George V and Queen Mary.

The 20th century was a time of great change in the life of the cathedral. The nave returned to liturgical use during World War I when Sunday evening services were held for the large number of servicemen from Britain and the Empire stationed in Winchester. Both World Wars and more recent conflicts have left their mark on the cathedral, with its important military memorials.

A huge increase in lay involvement occurred in the 1930s. The foundation of the Friends of Winchester Cathedral in 1931 was particularly influential. Then, several other bodies were formed with responsibility for various aspects of cathedral life and ministry. Amongst the first were the Broderers, who created the cathedral's pioneering embroideries under the direction of Louisa Pesel and Sybil Blunt. Today's specialist teams include the Guild of Voluntary Guides; those who exercise the ministry of welcome; library and Triforium Gallery helpers; flower arrangers; calligraphers; and the quaintly named 'Holy Dusters' and 'Brass Band', who assist the professional virgers in keeping the cathedral clean. This active participation of lay people in the life of the cathedral was the inspiration of Dean Selwyn, who also founded The Pilgrims' School, a double choir school whose pupils include both the cathedral choristers and the Winchester College Quiristers.

▲ Military memorials are an important feature of the cathedral. Two display cases in the south nave aisle contain books inscribed with the names of officers and men of the Royal Hampshire Regiment, killed in battle. The pages are regularly turned by an officer of the regiment.

▲ The George V window, by Hugh Easton, was a gift from the American people and was inaugurated by the US ambassador in 1938. In the top tier St George of England is flanked by Edward the Confessor and William the Conqueror; George V is depicted at the bottom right.

▲ The Triforium Gallery was opened in 1989 in order to display
some of the cathedral's many splendid art treasures.

◀ ▶ THE EPIPHANY CHAPEL
IS NOTABLE FOR ITS WINDOWS
DESIGNED BY EDWARD BURNE-
JONES AND CREATED BY THE
WILLIAM MORRIS WORKSHOP
(1907–9). THIS PANEL DEPICTS
THE ANNUNCIATION, THE ANGEL
GABRIEL TELLING THE VIRGIN
MARY THAT SHE IS TO BEAR A SON.

◀ ▲ The other windows portray the Visitation (Mary visits her cousin Elizabeth), the Nativity, and the Adoration of the Magi (the visit of the three kings, bearing gifts).

▲ CHRISTMAS IS AN IMPORTANT TIME FOR THE CATHEDRAL'S MUSICAL FOUNDATION.

▶ THE GIRLS' CHOIR WAS FOUNDED IN 1999, AND THE GIRL CHORISTERS JOIN THE LAY CLERKS (THE MEN SINGERS) TO BROADEN WINCHESTER CATHEDRAL'S MUSICAL TRADITION.

Music continues to play a vital role in cathedral worship. A series of distinguished musicians succeeded Samuel Sebastian Wesley as organist, and in 1949 Alwyn Surplice was appointed. He laid the foundations for the cathedral choir as we know it today. Under his successors the renown of Winchester's music has reached a wider public through the media of recording and broadcasting, and the mission of the cathedral has been extended by the choir's foreign tours. The cathedral's musical resources were enriched still further with the formation of a girls' choir in 1999.

Many exciting new initiatives have taken place in the past decades. The Education Centre gives thousands of schoolchildren an opportunity of learning about the life of a great cathedral. The Benedictine tradition of hospitality has been revived with the opening by HM Queen Elizabeth of the cathedral Visitors' Centre in 1993. The cathedral's links with other churches, beginning with Stavanger, were broadened in 1978 when Dean Michael Stancliffe renewed the ancient relationship with the monastery of Fleury at Saint-Benoît-sur-Loire, and have now expanded to include, as partners in mission, the cathedrals of Namirembe (Uganda), Newcastle-upon-Tyne, Rangoon, and Florence. The cathedral has developed its mission within the city and county and is host to many special services and events.

The fabric of the cathedral has received much-needed attention under a succession of cathedral architects with a background in conservation, and the work is monitored by a Fabric Committee of people who have recognized expertise in a wide variety of relevant fields. New works of art have been introduced into the cathedral.

▶ A MODERN PIETÀ (THE VIRGIN MARY HOLDING THE BODY OF HER CRUCIFIED SON) CARVED BY PETER EUGENE BALL IS DISPLAYED IN THE LADY CHAPEL.

Far-reaching changes occurred at the start of the
new millennium, with the drawing up of new Cathedral Statutes, with provision for lay representation on
Chapter and in a Cathedral Council to which the Chapter is accountable. Yet Winchester Cathedral continues
the primary purpose for which it has always existed,
as now defined in its Mission Statement: 'To make the
Cathedral more accessible as a place where God the
Holy Trinity meets all people and they may seek Him.'

▶ Barbara Hepworth's sculpture 'Construction (Crucifixion):
Homage to Mondrian' (1966) stands in Mirabel Close.

◀ Modern vestments: The
Very Revd. Michael Till, Dean
of Winchester, wearing a
purple chasuble designed by
Lucy Goffin.

▶ Large congregations at
Sunday services and at major
festivals require the nave to be
used for worship.

INDEX